Big Kids Coloring Book: Gray Scale Revolutionary City Architecture, Restored District, Williamsburg, VA Geographic Area

Gray-Scale Photographs to Add Your Own Color and Shading - Volume One

Photos by Dawn D. Boyer, Ph.D.

Published by:	Dawn D. Boyer, B.F.A., M.F.A. Ph.D. D. Boyer Consulting, Virginia Beach, VA 23464 www.DBoyerConsulting.com / Dawn.Boyer@dboyerconsulting.com
Book Copyright:	2016© by Dawn D. Boyer, Ph.D.
ISBN Numbers:	ISBN-13: 978-1532929021 ISBN-10: 1532929021 CS ID # 6231731

Author's Business Website	http://www.DBoyerConsulting.com
Amazon Author Page:	https://www.amazon.com/author/dawnboyer
Review Author's Books:	http://www.shelfari.com/DawnDeniseBoyer
Facebook Artist's Page:	http://www.Facebook.com/DawnBoyerArtist
Facebook Author's Page:	http://www.facebook.com/DawnBoyerAuthor
Facebook Business Page:	http://www.Facebook.com/DBoyerConsulting
Facebook Coloring Group Page:	https://www.facebook.com/groups/ColoringColoringColoring/
Google+ Business Page:	https://plus.google.com/112802498128568560150/about?hl=en
LinkedIn	http://www.linkedin.com/in/DawnBoyer
Twitter:	http://www.Twitter.com/Dawn_Boyer
Pinterest:	https://www.pinterest.com/dawnboyer/coloring-books-for-adults/

Find the Author's Artwork, Coloring Page Sample Packs, and Fine Art Illustrations for Sale on these Online Stores.

Etsy:	https://www.etsy.com/people/DawnDBoyer
Fine Art America	http://fineartamerica.com/profiles/dawn-boyer.html

INTRO

I grew up sketching, coloring, and drawing since I was five years old, so my artistic career and endeavors span five decades. My sketchbook(s) are overgrown with wild, wacky, and wonderful Zentangle Inspired Art (ZIA) work. When I realized there are folks who love finishing other artist's pen and ink artwork with their own personalized colors, it provided me the impetus to take the decades of art sketches and drawings that were gathering dust, and/or to create newer and better illustrations for others to color. I'm working on more pen and ink drawings of America's Revolutionary First Capital City (Williamsburg, Virginia geographic area) now. I completed a coloring book of delightful images of fairy houses and doors – first published in a 2015. The most recent volume of Fairy Houses and Fairy Doors (Vol. 2; 2015) came from fan requests for more fantasy fairy home images after publishing the first book. Then I created the Valentines Hearts A'Fire book, next was Feathers A'Flying book, and then Tantalizing Tangles – all while working on several other coloring books (Weddings, Vintage Toys, and pen illustrations of the Colonial Restoration area in the City of Williamsburg, Virginia.

When I started posting some of my Williamsburg Restoration Architecture pen drawings on Facebook, I had a few requests for gray-scale photos from those who love the area. Several folks requested pen and ink illustrations, and others asked about gray scale photos to add color to more realistic photos versus hand-drawn drawings. This book is a result for the gray-scale. My coloring books are all part of a series called "Big Kids Coloring Books" so when you search on Amazon or Barnes and Noble online, simply enter those words (using quotes helps) and my name for my entire collection.

Don't be scared to experiment with the drawings. There is no harm in playing around. That is the whole point of purchasing a coloring book! Whatever the artist's methods, choice of media, or preferred colors, these images should entertain the coloring co-artist for weeks or months.

These photos can be pulled out of the book to color (or use a craft knife to carefully slice the pages out of the spine). Don't be in a hurry to finish the book or complete the entire book before buying another. Pick the best, most appealing images and use your favorite colors, apply them in your preferred order and color intensity. Calm your mind and collect your peaceful feelings in your pursuit of beauty, peacefulness, and mindlessness. If you are stumped for complimentary colors or schemes, look for my books of colored mandalas and research the beautiful graphics for potential color combinations for use in coloring in your own creations.

Coloring-themed groups have popped up on social media in groups on Facebook (over 1,500 groups by January 2016). These include proprietary pages for coloring book artists showcasing their own books and artwork, groups created to show off colorists' finished work from purchased commercial books, and/or groups with members who share 'free' coloring images (search on 'color' or as the Brits (and their colony countries) spell it, 'colour'), as well as sample coloring pages or completed (fully colored) pieces showcased in Pinterest.

Please remember, photocopying the images in the book for 'personal use only' is permitted, but photocopying and sharing the uncolored pages with those who have not purchased the book or images separately (via online purchasing or retail stores) are practicing illegal copyright infringement and taking away from the artists' income. Be fair about sharing.

Enjoy and do follow my
artist's page on Facebook:
https://www.facebook.com/DawnBoyerArtist

Sample Pages

Sample Pages

Big Kids Coloring Book: Revolutionary City Architecture, Restored District, Williamsburg, Virginia Geographic Area Gray-Scale Photographs to Add Your Own Color and Shading

Big Kids Coloring Book: Revolutionary City Architecture, Restored District, Williamsburg, Virginia
Geographic Area Gray-Scale Photographs to Add Your Own Color and Shading

Big Kids Coloring Book: Revolutionary City Architecture, Restored District, Williamsburg, Virginia Geographic Area Gray-Scale Photographs to Add Your Own Color and Shading

Big Kids Coloring Book: Revolutionary City Architecture, Restored District, Williamsburg, Virginia Geographic Area Gray-Scale Photographs to Add Your Own Color and Shading

Big Kids Coloring Book: Revolutionary City Architecture, Restored District, Williamsburg, Virginia
Geographic Area Gray-Scale Photographs to Add Your Own Color and Shading

Big Kids Coloring Book: Revolutionary City Architecture, Restored District, Williamsburg, Virginia
Geographic Area Gray-Scale Photographs to Add Your Own Color and Shading

Big Kids Coloring Book: Revolutionary City Architecture, Restored District, Williamsburg, Virginia
Geographic Area Gray-Scale Photographs to Add Your Own Color and Shading

17

*Big Kids Coloring Book: Revolutionary City Architecture, Restored District, Williamsburg, Virginia
Geographic Area Gray-Scale Photographs to Add Your Own Color and Shading*

Big Kids Coloring Book: Revolutionary City Architecture, Restored District, Williamsburg, Virginia
Geographic Area Gray-Scale Photographs to Add Your Own Color and Shading

21

Big Kids Coloring Book: Revolutionary City Architecture, Restored District, Williamsburg, Virginia
Geographic Area Gray-Scale Photographs to Add Your Own Color and Shading

Big Kids Coloring Book: Revolutionary City Architecture, Restored District, Williamsburg, Virginia
Geographic Area Gray-Scale Photographs to Add Your Own Color and Shading

Big Kids Coloring Book: Revolutionary City Architecture, Restored District, Williamsburg, Virginia Geographic Area Gray-Scale Photographs to Add Your Own Color and Shading

Big Kids Coloring Book: Revolutionary City Architecture, Restored District, Williamsburg, Virginia
Geographic Area Gray-Scale Photographs to Add Your Own Color and Shading

33

Big Kids Coloring Book: Revolutionary City Architecture, Restored District, Williamsburg, Virginia Geographic Area Gray-Scale Photographs to Add Your Own Color and Shading

Big Kids Coloring Book: Revolutionary City Architecture, Restored District, Williamsburg, Virginia Geographic Area Gray-Scale Photographs to Add Your Own Color and Shading

Big Kids Coloring Book: Revolutionary City Architecture, Restored District, Williamsburg, Virginia
Geographic Area Gray-Scale Photographs to Add Your Own Color and Shading

Big Kids Coloring Book: Revolutionary City Architecture, Restored District, Williamsburg, Virginia
Geographic Area Gray-Scale Photographs to Add Your Own Color and Shading

Big Kids Coloring Book: Revolutionary City Architecture, Restored District, Williamsburg, Virginia Geographic Area Gray-Scale Photographs to Add Your Own Color and Shading

Big Kids Coloring Book: Revolutionary City Architecture, Restored District, Williamsburg, Virginia Geographic Area Gray-Scale Photographs to Add Your Own Color and Shading

Big Kids Coloring Book: Revolutionary City Architecture, Restored District, Williamsburg, Virginia
Geographic Area Gray-Scale Photographs to Add Your Own Color and Shading

Big Kids Coloring Book: Revolutionary City Architecture, Restored District, Williamsburg, Virginia
Geographic Area Gray-Scale Photographs to Add Your Own Color and Shading

*Big Kids Coloring Book: Revolutionary City Architecture, Restored District, Williamsburg, Virginia
Geographic Area Gray-Scale Photographs to Add Your Own Color and Shading*

Big Kids Coloring Book: Revolutionary City Architecture, Restored District, Williamsburg, Virginia Geographic Area Gray-Scale Photographs to Add Your Own Color and Shading

Big Kids Coloring Book: Revolutionary City Architecture, Restored District, Williamsburg, Virginia
Geographic Area Gray-Scale Photographs to Add Your Own Color and Shading

Big Kids Coloring Book: Revolutionary City Architecture, Restored District, Williamsburg, Virginia
Geographic Area Gray-Scale Photographs to Add Your Own Color and Shading

Big Kids Coloring Book: Revolutionary City Architecture, Restored District, Williamsburg, Virginia
Geographic Area Gray-Scale Photographs to Add Your Own Color and Shading

Big Kids Coloring Book: Revolutionary City Architecture, Restored District, Williamsburg, Virginia
Geographic Area Gray-Scale Photographs to Add Your Own Color and Shading

*Big Kids Coloring Book: Revolutionary City Architecture, Restored District, Williamsburg, Virginia
Geographic Area Gray-Scale Photographs to Add Your Own Color and Shading*

Big Kids Coloring Book: Revolutionary City Architecture, Restored District, Williamsburg, Virginia
Geographic Area Gray-Scale Photographs to Add Your Own Color and Shading

Big Kids Coloring Book: Revolutionary City Architecture, Restored District, Williamsburg, Virginia
Geographic Area Gray-Scale Photographs to Add Your Own Color and Shading

About the Author / Artist / Photographer
Dawn D. Boyer, Ph.D.

Dawn D. Boyer, Ph.D. has been drawing since she was five years old, and would color her father's office stationery with crayons to create brilliantly hued paper for her art projects. She received her first acrylic paint set in 1973 and promptly confused and frustrated the art teacher by finishing class projects in hours versus days. She won her first art award in the 9th grade at her high school (Highland Springs High School, Virginia; 1972) for a large poster design that today would be called 'Zentangle Inspired Art' (ZIA).

She attended Virginia Commonwealth University's Bachelor of Art Program and then re-engaged later at Radford University where she earned her BFA in Graphic Design and Illustration. She later returned to Virginia Commonwealth University to earn her Master's Degree in Adult Education and completed her Doctorate of Philosophy in Education Old Dominion University (Norfolk, VA).

Over the years she has developed a distinctive style for her pen and ink illustrations of old barns and houses, as well as the first Nation's Capital, the City of Williamsburg, Virginia, and the restored colonial area and it's beautiful restored buildings and other architectural portraiture. She works in mixed-media, using recycled magazines to create 3-D images of stylistic animals and mandalas, as well as using childhood craft processes (bubble-gum chains, paper footballs, and quilling techniques) to create non-traditional and sophisticated, woven paper baskets.

Her doodling and art sketches started in high school before it was known as the style as 'Zentangle Inspired Artwork' (Zentangle® is a registered name for a particular type of artwork now based on specific doodle patterns in a variety of combinations).

She is the author of 103+ books on the topics of business, career search practices, mandala books for hypnotherapy and meditation, coloring books for adults, women and gender studies, and quotes for self-improvement ("2,000+" & "3,000+" series), as well as genealogy and family lineage. Eighty of her books can be found on Amazon.com (as of 2016). She assists other authors, including Ph.D. graduates, publish their manuscripts in the print-on-demand commercial market and also has a series of books entitled: "Interview with An Artist." The interview books compile artists' interviews with photos of the artist's work to assist the artists in marketing and branding their work to an international marketplace. She is also active in writing business-related stories for the local Virginian Pilot's Inside Business weekly, "Ask the Expert" column, as well as stories in national American Business Journals columns.

She finished her doctor of philosophy studies May 2013 at Old Dominion University in Norfolk, VA in Education (major in Occupational & Technical Studies, with a minor concentration in Training & Development within Human Resources). Her dissertation is entitled, 'Competencies of Human Resources Practitioners within the Government Contracting Industry,' which identifies unique KSAs for Human Resources Managers working for federal level government contracting companies.

Dr. Boyer has been an entrepreneur and business owner for 14+ years, with a past successful business in Richmond, VA, currently in her own consulting firm, and as a business partner with her husband in Virginia Beach, VA. She also mentors entrepreneurs as part of the federal government's Small Business Administration SCORE program. Her background experience is 22+ years in the Human Resources field, of which 12+ years are within the Federal & Defense Contracting industry.

Business Website   www.DBoyerConsulting.com

LinkedIn Profile   www.LinkedIn.com/in/DawnBoyer

Twitter   www.Twitter.com/Dawn_Boyer

YouTube   www.youtube.com/user/DawnDeniseBoyer

Facebook Artist's Page   www.Facebook.com/DawnBoyerArtist

D. Boyer Consulting, Virginia Beach, VA 23464
http://dboyerconsulting.com / Dawn@DBoyerConsulting.com

To see how others are coloring Dawn Boyer's Pen and Ink Artwork, visit:
https://www.facebook.com/groups/ColoringPagesByDawnBoyer/

Big Kids Coloring Book: Revolutionary City Architecture, Restored District, Williamsburg, Virginia
Geographic Area Gray-Scale Photographs to Add Your Own Color and Shading

About the Book

The artist, Dawn D. Boyer, Ph.D., has produced a compilation of delightful photographs in this coloring book which allows you, the colorist, to use your imagination in coloring those pictures and pages in multiple ways with your choice of media. In this book you will find dozens of photos you color and practice your shading, contouring, and coloring for a one-of-a-kind colonial-era architectural portrait. All of the page in this book were created from the artist's photographs.

The book is standard publisher paper (60# weight) and non-perforated paper with glue binding. Colorists can choose to use dry media (crayons or colored pencils) or wet media (markers, gel pens, or paints) to complete the beautiful and rich photographs in the gray scale pages.

What can you do with the book once you have finished? Once the designs in this book are colored – give the books as gifts, use pages as scrapbook background art, create greeting cards, or use the designs and use in multi-media art. The possibilities are endless!

Enjoy and connect with the artist's page on Facebook to post and show YOUR coloring results!
https://www.facebook.com/groups/ColoringPagesByDawnBoyer/

++
KEY SEARCH TERMS FOR DAWN'S BOOKS ON AMAZON: Adult Coloring Book, Architectural Illustrations, Artist's renderings, artwork, balance, Barns, Big Kids Coloring Book, bugs, butterflies, calming, celebration, channel, circle, co-artist, City of Williamsburg Virginia, color, Coloring Book, colors, colour, colouring, colouring book, colours, composition, concentration, consciousness, contemplate, cosmos, crab, creation, Dawn.Boyer@me.com, de-stress, designs, dolphin, doodle, doodles, Drawing, drawings, emotions, heart, hearts, fae, fairies, fairy, fairy doors, fairy houses, fauna, feathers, feathers a'flying, feathers aflying, fish, flora, forest, Forgotten Places, forms, hidden animals, hearts, Hearts A'Fire, hidden shapes, Illustration, imagination, jellyfish, joy, Kaleidoscope, life, lionfish, lived, lobster, love, loving, magical, mandala, mermaids, mother earth, mystical, mystical creatures, nature, ocean, Old Barns, Old Houses, pattern, peace, pen and ink, powers, psyche, psychological, psychology, psychotherapy, re-balancing, reflecting, relax, relaxation, sand painting, sea, self, self-hypnosis, self-remembering, shading, shark, shipwreck, space, spirits, spiritual, state-of-being, strengths, sub-conscious, sugar skulls, symbolic, tangles, tantalizing, therapy, thought, transcendental, tropical, undersea, universe, valentine, valentines, wakefulness, well-being, Williamsburg Virginia Geographic Area, wisdom, Zen, Zendala, Zentangles
++

To see sample illustrations of some of the images included in this book before you purchase, use Amazon's "Peek Between the Covers" feature for Pages 3 and 4 illustration samples.

CPSIA information can be obtained
at www.ICGtesting.com
Printed in the USA
BVOW10s2137210816

459738BV00006B/58/P